even among these rocks

Steven D. Purcell

First edition 2000
05 04 03 02 01 00 7 6 5 4 3 2 1
ISBN 0-9535757-1-3

Published by Piquant
PO Box 83, Carlisle, CA3 9GR, United Kingdom
E-mail: info@piquant.net
Website: www.piquant.net

Copublished in the United States by Paraclete Press
Brewster, Massachusetts, USA
E-mail: mail@paracletepress.com
Website: www.paracletepress.com

ISBN 1-55725-273-4

Cover design by Sam Hill, Vertical Seconds.
Printed and bound in Singapore

for Jack and Mary Purcell
   my parents and my friends

Table of Contents

Foreword

FOR CHRISTIANS, THERE IS ONLY ONE ROAD TO TRAVEL, THE ROAD BLAZED BY JESUS, THE JESUS' ROAD ("I AM THE WAY..." JN. 14.6). BUT THE WAYS IN WHICH WE WALK, THE EXPERIENCES WE ACCUMULATE, THE PEOPLE WE MEET ALONG THE WAY ARE WONDERFULLY DIVERSE: THE ODD MISFIT WHO BECOMES A BEST FRIEND, A PAINFUL STUBBED TOE, A SKINSOAKING RAIN, THE DELICATE SCENT OF NEWLY-LEAVED COTTONWOODS ON A SPRING MORNING, LATE NIGHT FATIGUE COMPOUNDED BY BLACK DOUBT, A SUDDENLY ILLUMINATED TEXT FROM ISAIAH, AND ASSORTED UNCLASSIFIABLE TEMPTATIONS, JOYS AND PRAYERS. THERE ARE AS MANY WAYS OF WALKING THIS WAY AS THERE ARE PILGRIMS WHO WALK IT. MOST OF THEM ARE WORTH TALKING ABOUT.

OUR EXPERIENCES "ON THE ROAD" MAKE FOR TERRIFIC CONVERSATION AND PROFOUND MEDITATION, CEMENTING FRIENDSHIPS AND EVOKING LOVE AMONG FELLOW TRAVELLERS. EVEN THOUGH A COMMON BELIEVING OBEDIENCE PUTS US ON THIS ROAD THAT WE WALK (OR RUN!) IN COMMON, NO TWO PEOPLE DO IT IN EXACTLY THE SAME WAY—CHRISTIANS DON'T MARCH IN PRECISE FORMATION. IN FACT, THERE IS NOTHING IN LIFE THAT IS LESS SUSCEPTIBLE TO STEREOTYPE THAN A CHRISTIAN WHO FOLLOWS JESUS ON "THE WAY." EVERY CHRISTIAN IS AN ORIGINAL; THE HOLY SPIRIT DOESN'T GO IN FOR COPYING OLD MASTERS; EVERY SOUL IS A NEW CREATION. SINS AFTER AWHILE ALL BEGIN TO LOOK AND SOUND ALIKE (THE DEVIL NEVER SEEMS ABLE TO INSPIRE ANYTHING BEYOND CHEAP REPRODUCTIONS). BUT EVERY VIRTUE, EVERY ACT OF FAITH, EVERY VENTURE INTO OBEDIENCE IS ONE-OF-KIND. THE CHRISTIAN LIFE, EXCEPT IN THE OVERALL SENSE THAT IT DERIVES FROM JESUS' LIFE AND IS COMPOSED ON THE PLOT OF HOLY SCRIPTURE, IS UNPREDICTABLE IN ITS FREE FALL THROUGH THE ATMOSPHERE OF GRACE. THE HAPPY RESULT IS THAT WE, THE COMPANY OF JESUS-FOLLOWERS, ARE SURROUNDED BY STORIES AND SONGS, POEMS AND PAINTINGS THAT ENCOURAGE, ENTERTAIN AND ENRICH THE JOURNEY.

STEVEN PURCELL'S LENTEN JOURNEY IS NOW ANOTHER OFFERING. HE EVOKES OUR RESPONSES AT MANY LEVELS TO WAKE US UP TO SO MUCH OF WHAT SOME OF US WITH OUR VARIOUS PREOCCUPATIONS AND BLIND-SPOTS MISS. HE EMPLOYS AND COMBINES ELEGANT CALLIGRAPHY, SUBTLE WATERCOLORS, SELECTED POETS, HEART-DEEP PRAYERS, PAINTINGS AND DRAWINGS OF THE MASTERS, HOLY SCRIPTURE, AND HIS OWN MEDITATIONS ON THE JOURNEY TO HEIGHTEN NOT ONLY OUR ALIVENESS AS WE JOURNEY BUT OUR AWARENESS OF CHRISTIAN LIVES, OUR LIVES, AS SPIRIT-MADE ARTFORMS ON THE JOURNEY. FOLLOWING JESUS ON THE WAY IS NOT ONLY A MATTER OF FINDING OUR WAY HOME; IT IS ALSO STAYING AWAKE AND RESPONSIVE TO EVERYTHING THAT CAN BE SEEN, SMELLED, TOUCHED, AND HEARD ALONG THE WAY AS WE FOLLOW JESUS IN THE COMPANY OF HIS FRIENDS WHO BECOME OUR FRIENDS. WELCOME STEVEN PURCELL AS A WIDEAWAKE, SPIRIT-RESPONSIVE FRIEND ON THE JOURNEY.

EUGENE H PETERSON
PROFESSOR EMERITUS OF SPIRITUAL THEOLOGY
REGENT COLLEGE, VANCOUVER B.C. CANADA

Preface

The idea for this book began with a decision to participate as fully as I could in the forty days of Lent. The themes which make up the seven chapters which follow are the collective result of that journey. They are not original themes. While many others have dealt with them and given their own accounts in one form or another, this book is a personal record of what I saw and heard. I do not expect it will perfectly reflect the Lenten experience of everyone, but it is my hope that others will recognize these vignettes from their own experiences of poverty and redemption and be drawn into communion with the God of grace.

There is an intentional order to the following chapters, but I do not mean to imply by this order that the journey of Lent—or the journey of faith—is a linear ascent toward a static goal. Nor do I wish to convey the idea that the journey described is a map for others to follow. What is important is how the content and structure of the book suggests a movement forward, but forward in such a way that the traveller is consistently led back to his or her beginning. The Lenten pilgrimage is not about developing greater spiritual competence, nor achieving mystical enlightenment. Rather, it is an exercise in following. Specifically, it means following Christ and—in that journey of faith—discovering the truth about ourselves and the largeness of God's love.

Though it was born of my own experience, this book is the product of many friendships. During the course of its development it was my privilege to live alongside a faithful community of friends at Regent College, Vancouver. It was in the context of those relationships that the following words and images came together, first in my own life and then onto the page. This project would not have reached its present form without the support and genuine encouragement of my academic supervisors Loren Wilkinson and Dal Schindell, to whom I am deeply grateful. I owe a special debt of thanks to Pieter Kwant (Piquant Publishing) for his enthusiastic support of this project from its conceptual beginnings and his positive and professional manner which continued to the end. I would also like to thank my parents Jack and Mary Purcell, who by their faith and friendship have taught me most about the Father's grace.

Steven D. Purcell
Vancouver

The Invitation

The Lord is compassionate and gracious
    slow to anger, abounding in love
He will not always accuse,
    nor will he harbor his anger forever;
he does not treat us as our sins deserve
    or repay us according to our iniquities
For as high as the heavens are above the earth,
    so great is his love for those who fear him;
As far as the east is from the west,
    so far has he removed our transgressions from us.
As a father has compassion on his children,
    so the Lord has compassion on those who fear him;
for he knows how we are formed,
    he remembers that we are dust.
As for man, his days are like grass,
    he flourishes like a flower of the field;
the wind blows over it and it is gone,
    and its place remembers it no more.
But from everlasting to everlasting
    the Lord's love is with those who fear him,
    and his righteousness with their children's children —

Psalm 103:8-17

Come to me, all you who are weary
and burdened, and I will give you
rest. Take my yoke upon you and learn
from me, for I am gentle and humble
in heart, and you will find rest for
your souls. For my yoke is easy and
my burden is light.

Matthew 11:28-30

of the Holy Trinity and it is Christ, who by his incarnation, leads us there. George MacDonald describes this movement well when he writes that "Christ is the way out, and the way in: the way from slavery, conscious or unconscious, into liberty; the way from the unhomeliness of things to the home we desire but do not know; the way from the stormy skirts of the Father's garments to the peace of his bosom." Our beginning is defined by the love of God, and as St. Augustine prayed, "our hearts are restless until they find their rest in Thee." By identifying himself with us in our humanity, Christ redeems our humanity and thereby enables us to be ourselves authentically, for the first time. The process of our redemption is never the result of courageous forays into ourselves, but rather, the life-long process of the Son drawing us out of ourselves and into the community of his triune life and the life around us.

As we respond to the invitation of Lent we should expect to face two important realities. First, we will be led to remember the life of Christ including his ministry, sacrifice and resurrection. But second, we will be led to face ourselves. The precariousness of this twofold reckoning is described in lines from T.S. Eliot's poem "Ash Wednesday":

Teach us to care and not to care
Teach us to sit still
Even among these rocks
Our peace in His will.

~T.S. Eliot

Lent is a pilgrimage which Christ personally invites us to make. The journey is not an adventure for tourists who wish to capture snapshots of spiritual insight, but rather an invitation which comes from Christ and draws us to Christ. What is unique about this personal invitation is that Christ invites us to make a journey that he himself has already made. It is the nature of his grace not merely to call us from the outside, but actually to draw us from within. In one sense, the Lenten journey is our journey home into the community

even among these rocks

As Eliot points out, the journey of remembering is no place for falsehood. In Lent we are encouraged to care for those things which ultimately matter and to leave behind those things which inhibit our participation in the life of God and the life around us. As we remember with honesty the way things are—who Christ is and who we are as subjects of his redemption—we will learn to "sit still," our peace in his will. This is the invitation of Lent—to move through the wilderness of self-deception into the truth of Christ.

Being a Lenten traveler inevitably requires leaving behind those things which have become "home" to us. It involves a separation from the securities and attachments of our life for the sake of discovering the truth about ourselves and the Lord who calls us. Nevertheless, having left behind our securities we are not left to cajole, lament or flatter our way home. No, the offensive paradox of the season is that we're simply asked to respond to the loving invitation of Christ. Any movement we make toward Christ will always be an act of response. And every step taken toward him confirms the mystery that our journey into the community of the triune God is our journey home.

This painting by the Russian iconographer Andrew Rublev (†1430) depicts the Holy Trinity with the Son in the center, the Father to the left and the Holy Spirit on the right. Within the composition the figures are seated around three sides of the table, with an open place before the viewer. By this openness we are invited to take our place at the table and join the fellowship of God. In terms of perspective it is also interesting that the vanishing point appears to be placed where we are (rather than in the distance), and opens beyond us into the ever-widening life of the Trinity. By these two compositional details alone, Rublev's icon echoes the invitation of Lent: That we might move beyond the confines of ourselves into the life and infinite possibility of the triune God.

Love bade me welcome.

Words by
GEORGE HERBERT.

Music by
R. VAUGHAN WILLIAMS.

Almighty and everlasting God, who hatest nothing that thou hast made, and dost forgive the sins of all them that are penitent;

Create and make in us new and contrite hearts, that we worthily lamenting our sins, and acknowledging our wretchedness, may obtain of thee, the God of all mercy, perfect remission and forgiveness; through Jesus Christ our Lord.

Amen~

Love bade me welcome; yet my soul drew back,
    Guilty of dust and sin.
But quick-eyed love, observing me grow slack
    From my first entrance in,
Drew nearer to me, sweetly questioning
    If I lacked anything.

"A guest" I answered, "worthy to be here."
    Love said, "You shall be he."
"I, the unkind, ungrateful: Ah my dear,
    I cannot look on Thee."
Love took my hand and smiling did reply,
    "Who made the eye but I?"

"Truth, Lord, but I have marred them: let my shame
    Go where it doth deserve."
"And know you not," says love, "who bore the blame?"
    "My dear, then I will serve."
"You must sit down," says Love, "and taste my meat."
    So I did sit and eat.

The Desert of Temptation

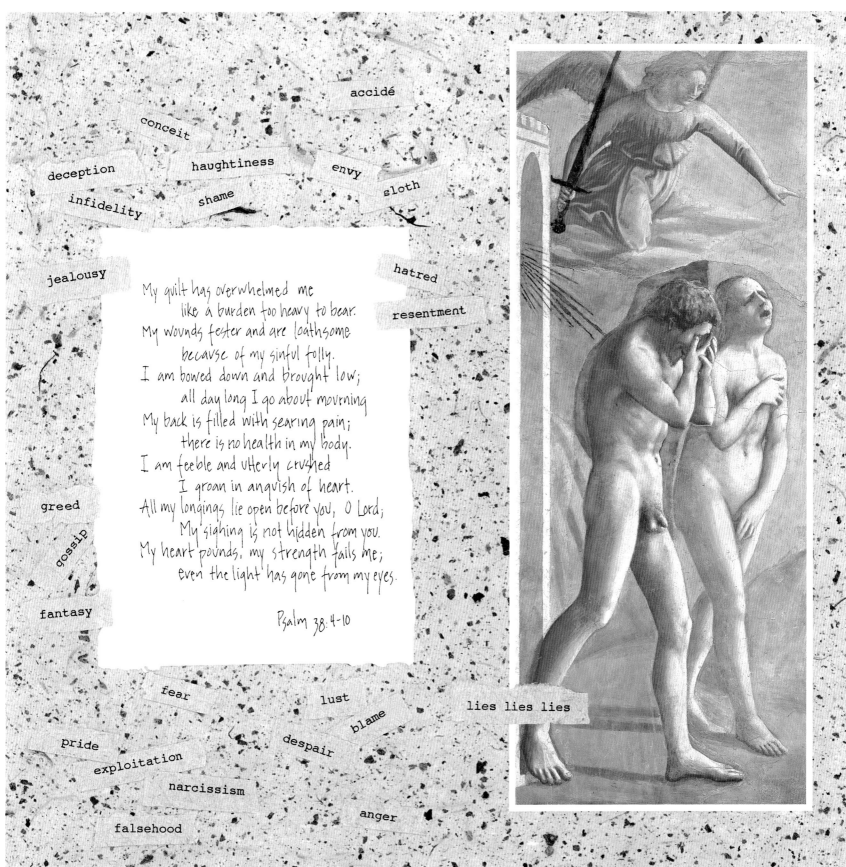

accidé

conceit

deception   haughtiness   envy

infidelity   shame   sloth

jealousy   hatred

resentment

My guilt has overwhelmed me
          like a burden too heavy to bear.
My wounds fester and are loathsome
          because of my sinful folly.
I am bowed down and brought low;
          all day long I go about mourning
My back is filled with searing pain;
          there is no health in my body.
I am feeble and utterly crushed
          I groan in anguish of heart.
All my longings lie open before you, O Lord;
          My sighing is not hidden from you.
My heart pounds, my strength fails me;
          even the light has gone from my eyes.

                                        Psalm 38:4-10

greed

gossip

fantasy

fear   lust

                    blame

pride   despair

exploitation

narcissism

                    anger

falsehood

lies lies lies

Then Jesus was led by the Spirit into the desert to be tempted by the devil. After fasting forty days and forty nights, he was hungry. The tempter came to him and said, "If you are the Son of God, tell these stones to become bread."

Jesus answered, "It is written: 'Man does not live on bread alone, but on every word that comes from the mouth of God.'"

Then the devil took him to the holy city and had him stand on the highest point of the temple. "If you are the Son of God," he said, "throw yourself down. For it is written:

"'He will command his angels concerning you, and they will lift you up in their hands, so that you will not strike your foot against a stone.'"

Jesus answered him, "It is written: 'Do not put the Lord your God to the test.'"

Again, the devil took him to a very high mountain and showed him all the kingdoms of the world and their splendor. "All this I will give you," he said, "if you will bow down and worship me."

Jesus said to him, "Away from me Satan! For it is written: 'Worship the Lord your God and serve him only.'"

Then the devil left him, and angels came and attended him.

Matthew 4: 1-12

Throughout biblical and church history the people of God are frequently found living in the desert. The desert is the geographic setting of the Exodus, Christ's temptation and home to the desert fathers of the fourth century. But the desert has also been used to symbolize the geography of the human heart. With desert metaphors we are able to express the barrenness, aridity and vulnerability often felt within our souls. Many people have purposefully entered the desert in order to submit themselves to physical as well as spiritual conditions that expose the soul. On the other hand, many of us find ourselves in spiritual deserts against our wills. Nevertheless, the effects are the same: The desert exposes and lays bare. In it we are tempted and suffer as Christ was tempted and suffered. The significance of the desert experience, chosen or not, is that by it God is able to reveal the true condition of the human heart. The wild, trackless and vulnerable experience of the spiritual desert exposes our personal vulnerability to all sorts of evil and our absolute dependence on God's grace.

As the first steps of Christ's ministry began in the desert, so too our Lenten journey home begins there. Having accepted Christ's invitation to follow him, our journey has begun.

In our identification with Christ the spirit leads us into the desert, bringing us face to face with the reality of temptation and our vulnerability to sin. It is here that we realize that only he can forgive and save us from ourselves. If we miss this first step, we miss the heart of Lent.

The two-part focus of Lent involves having a renewed vision of Christ's passion and a fresh understanding of our own sin. The desert is a dangerous place, full of illusions and deceptive mirages. We're tempted in the desert to focus on anything that will distract us from the barrenness of our souls. T.S. Eliot was aware of this temptation when he wrote in "Ash Wednesday" of "struggling with the devil of the stairs who wears the deceitful face of hope and despair." When encountering the evil which lies hidden within ourselves, there is always the risk of trivializing our guilt on one hand or digressing into self-devouring despair on the other. If we're exclusively distracted by our sin and fail to keep before us the vision of Christ, we'll progress no further than despair; depression at worst. Conversely, if we think grace will allow us to receive the mercy of Christ without having honestly faced our poverty, then we risk being duped by the devil who wears the "deceitful face of hope." To see Christ is to see the God who is full of mercy and whose nature it is to forgive. But this vision presupposes knowledge of our need for mercy and forgiveness in the first place. The Lenten journey represents an encounter between our misery and God's mercy, our guilt and his forgiveness.

The Lord's Supper is the Church's sacramental reminder of this encounter. As surely as the bread and wine communicate to us Christ's grace and forgiveness, so eating his flesh and drinking his blood reminds us of our comprehensive guilt.

At every Lord's Supper we acknowledge the true dimension of our lives and are led to repent. As Bernard of Clairvaux reminds us, "To meet the eyes of Jesus is to see one's sinfulness and be forgiven simultaneously."

When Christ is led by the Spirit into the desert, he is tempted in the vulnerability of his humanity about his relationship to his Father. In the first temptation he is enticed to exercise power on his own behalf rather than trust himself to the care of his Father. In the second temptation Jesus is persuaded to "make use of God" rather than serve him. At the third and last temptation, Christ is coerced to promote himself — to commit idolatry. It helps us to consider the common element in each response of Jesus. In each temptation is the appeal to live self-sufficiently — to rely on his own devices for securing power, pleasure and position. When Jesus recites the Torah he is not merely parroting magical maxims. The victory of his response is that with each temptation he remains faithful to his relationship with the Father. Each temptation is an attack of this relationship. Each response of Jesus honors this relationship. Such obedience reveals the truth that Life, as created by the triune God, is fundamentally relational. Sin, therefore, is the rejection of our intrinsic relatedness to God and the rest of his creation. We live either obediently within relationship to the Trinity, or alienated in the hell of our own disobedience.

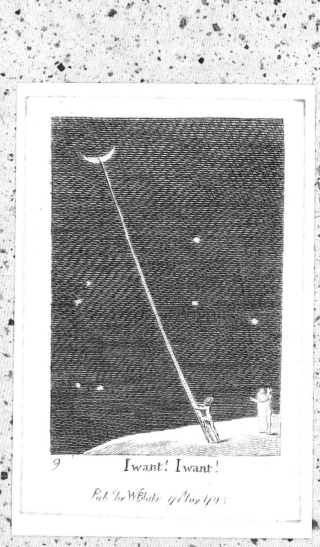

9   I want! I want!

Fab.r by W Blake if May 1793

William Blake's simple etching illustrates the point that sin is never the solitary escapade of desire that we imagine it to be, but more fundamentally the rejection of our relational identity. The ladder depicts an apparently innocuous ascent. Where the ladder will lead is perhaps immaterial. What is at stake are the relationships which are affected by his act. What we see in Blake's etching is how movements away from our neighbor and toward our own desires in the spirit of "I want, I want," neglect the communal image of God impressed on our being.

I am not worthy, Master and Lord, that you should come beneath the roof of my soul: yet since you in your love toward all wish to dwell in me, in boldness I come. You command, Open the gates — which you alone have forged; and you will come in with love toward all as is your nature; you will come in and enlighten my darkened reason. I believe that you will do this: for you did not send away the harlot that came to you with tears; nor cast out the repentant publican; nor reject the thief who acknowledged your kingdom; nor forsake the repentant persecutor, a yet greater act, but all of those who came to you in repentance, were counted in the band of your friends, who alone abide blessed forever, now, and unto the endless ages. Amen.

— St. John Chrysostom (c. 347 - 407)

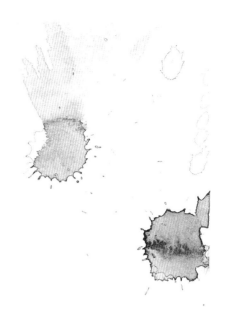

Batter my heart, three-personed God, for you
As yet but knock, breathe, shine and seek to mend;
That I may rise and stand, o'erthrow me and bend
Your force, to break, blow, burn, and make me new.
I, like unusurped town, to another due,
Labor to admit You, but Oh, to no end!
Reason, Your viceroy in me, me should defend,
But it captivated, and proves weak or untrue.
Yet dearly I love you, and would be loved fain,
But am betrothed unto Your enemy:
Divorce me, untie or break that knot again,
Take me to you, imprison me, never shall be free,
Nor ever chaste, except You ravish me.

— John Donne

Uncovering Illusions

Georges Rouault
Don't We All Wear Makeup?

Blessed are the man and woman
    who have grown beyond their greed
    and have put an end to their hatred
    and no longer nourish illusions.
But they delight in the way of grace
    and keep their hearts open day and night.
They are like trees planted near flowing rivers
    which bear fruit when they are ready.
Their leaves will not fall or whither
    Everything they do will succeed.

        Psalm 1
        trans. from the 8th-3rd cent. B.C.

When he had finished speaking, he said to Simon, "Put out into deep water, and let down the nets for a catch." Simon answered, "Master, we've worked hard all night and haven't caught anything. But because you say so, I will let down the nets."

When they had done so, they caught such a large number of fish that their nets began to break. So they signaled their partners in the other boat to come and help them, and they came and filled both boats so full that they began to sink.

When Simon Peter saw this, he fell at Jesus' knees and said, "Go away from me, Lord; I am a sinful man!" For he and all his companions were astonished at the catch of fish they had taken, and so were James and John, the sons of Zebedee, Simon's partners.

Then Jesus said to Simon, "Don't be afraid; from now on you will catch men." So they pulled their boats up on shore, left everything and followed him.

Luke 5:4-11

Peter's initial response to Jesus is one of politeness and accommodation. Quickly, however, he discovers that something far beyond mere appearances is at work. This is not just a fortuitous catch of fish and neither is it a lucky guess on the part of Jesus. Peter is encountering a person of authority. In a single moment Peter realizes that he could no longer maintain the pretense of accepting Jesus as a wise teacher, a dispenser of ideas or a kindly friend. No longer could he hide behind his fisherman's persona. When Peter stands face to face with Jesus and realizes Christ's authority and righteousness, he is no longer able to maintain the status quo. Peter encounters the Living Lord and is shaken to the core.

When we confront the righteous presence of Christ, our masks and illusions are quickly removed and unveiled. Like Peter, we too are moved to demand passively or aggressively that God and others "go away" from us. W.H. Auden describes the terror of having our masks removed with these words:

> We would rather be ruined than changed
> We would rather die in our dread
> Than climb the cross of the moment
> And see our illusions die.

Masks and illusions are intimately bound together with sin because they are precisely that which allows us to have our own way while keeping our consciences sufficiently distanced from the scrutiny of God and others. The problem is not that parts of our inner selves are covered and hid from public view. After all, it was God who gave appropriate coverings to the couple expelled from the garden. Problems arise when these coverings become facades which hide the truth about ourselves — or when we believe the masks are really us. The longer our masks remain fixed, the more alienated we become from ourselves and others.

Peter's response to Jesus — "Go away from me!" — is motivated by more than astonishment at a large catch of fish. His reaction is that of a person who would rather be ruined than have his illusions die. All that Peter has believed of himself is brought into question by the presence of Christ. As Christ did with Peter, so the Holy Spirit approaches us in our illusory worlds — invoking terror. When we encounter the Spirit in the way Peter encountered Jesus, we fear being stripped of the masks and illusions that have given a sense of security. But as he did with Peter, Jesus says to us: "Fear not." Only Jesus has the authority to say the words "fear not" to us at the moment of our unmasking, for the reason that he alone knows us as we really are and loves us anyway. Furthermore, only God's love is able to redeem the poverty that we so desparately seek to hide.

In Scripture both judgment and the Holy Spirit are expressed with metaphors of "fire." Eliot portrays how the soul is consumed by either the fire of judgment or the fire of the Spirit Either way we are consumed. The flame of the Holy Spirit burns through the illusory walls of our self-protection and exposes not only our secret sins but also, and more profoundly the brokenness and poverty of our lives. It is by this flame though, that we live. For, it is the love of the triune God which consumes our self-deception, so that we might live before him as free and honest persons.

The dove descending breaks the air
With flame of incandescent terror
Of which the tongues declare
The one discharge from sin and error.
The only help, or else despair
         Lies in the choice of pyre or pyre
         To be redeemed from fire by fire.

Who then devised the torment? Love.
Love is the unfamiliar Name
Behind the hands that wove
The intolerable shirt of flame
Which human power cannot remove.
         We only live, only suspire
         Consumed by either fire or fire.

                    T.S. Eliot
                    "Little Gidding"

Georges Rouault
The Wounded Clown 1

An indelible impression was made on Rouault when he happened upon a circus caravan and quietly witnessed an old clown sitting at his trailer darning his glittery costume. What struck Rouault and initiated a long series of paintings around the circus theme was the contrast between the costume and make-up worn by the clown and the "infinite sadness" that rested just below the paint and glitter. "I have seen clearly" says Rouault, "that the 'clown' was I, was us, almost all of us . . . That sumptuous sequin covered costume is given to us by life, we are all clowns to a greater or lesser extent, we all wear a 'sequin covered costume,' but if someone surprises us as I have surprised the old clown, oh! Who would then dare say that he has not been overwhelmed, down to the pit of his stomach, by an immense pity." As a painter, Rouault was determined to reveal the soul of his subjects on their countenance, be they kings, prostitutes or clowns. He writes, "the greater he (the individual) is and the more he's glorified by humanity, the more I fear for his soul . . . ."

Because of your all-embracing, wonderful plan
which you have carried out in our regard,
we give you thanks and glorify you ceaselessly
in your church which you have redeemed
through the precious blood of your Christ.
With open mouths and faces unveiled
we present you with praise and honour
gratitude and adoration
to your living, holy, and life-giving name,
now and always
and forever and ever.
Amen.

The Anaphoras of Addai and Mari

The Abiding Presence

When my heart was grieved
    and my spirit embittered
I was senseless and ignorant;
    I was a brute beast before you
Yet I am always with you;
    you hold me by my right hand.
You guide me with your counsel,
    and afterward you will take me into glory.
Whom have I in heaven but you?
    And earth has nothing I desire besides you.
My flesh and my heart may fail,
    but God is the strength of my heart
    and my portion forever.

Those who are far from you will perish;
    you destroy all who are unfaithful to you.
But as for me, it is good to be near God.
    I have made the sovereign Lord my refuge;
    I will tell of all your deeds.

                    Psalm 73:21-28

There was a man who had two sons. The younger one said to his father, "Father, give me my share of the estate." So he divided his property between them.

Not long after that, the younger son got together all he had, set off for a distant country and there squandered his wealth in wild living. After he had spent everything, there was a severe famine in that whole country, and he began to be in need. So he went and hired himself out to a citizen of that country, who sent him to his fields to feed pigs. He longed to fill his stomach with the pods that the pigs were eating, but no one gave him anything.

When he came to his senses, he said, "How many of my father's hired men have food to spare, and here I am starving to death! I will set out and go back to my father and say to him: Father, I have sinned against heaven and against you. I am no longer worthy to be called your son; make me like one of your hired men." So he got up and went to his father.

But while he was still a long way off, his father saw him and was filled with compassion for him; he ran to his son, threw his arms around him and kissed him. Then the son said to him, "Father, I have sinned against heaven and against you. I am no longer worthy to be called your son."

But the father said to his servants, "Quick! Bring the best robe and put it on him. Put a ring on his finger and sandals on his feet. Bring the fattened calf and kill it. Let's have a feast and celebrate. For this son of mine was dead and is alive again; he was lost and is found." So they began to celebrate.

Meanwhile the older brother was in the field. When he came near the house, he heard music and dancing. So he called one of the servants and asked him what was going on. "Your brother has come," he replied, "and your father has killed the fattened calf because he has him back safe and sound."

The older brother became angry and refused to go in. So his father went out and pleaded with him. But he answered his father, "Look! All these years I've been slaving for you and never disobeyed your orders. Yet you never gave me even a young goat so I could celebrate with my friends. But when this son of yours who has squandered your property with prostitutes comes home, you kill the fattened calf for him!"

"My son," the father said, "you are always with me, and everything I have is yours. But we had to celebrate and be glad, because this brother of yours was dead and is alive again; he was lost and is found."

Luke 15:11-31

The story of the lost son is first and foremost the story of a compassionate father. In Rembrandt's interpretation of the story it is the loving presence of the father, surrounding the broken son, that captures the heart of the parable. It is the son who lost everything that discovers the open arms of his father and in that sufficient enclosure of love finds "presence." Perhaps nowhere else is the homeward journey of the broken and burdened so beautifully articulated. Rembrandt portrays the son so as to suggest a long absence from home. His garments are worn and spare, he wears nothing on his feet, his one-time wealth is replaced by a wooden staff now thrown to the side, and his face—detailed with anguish— looks particularly weathered from exposure. The older brother (who incidentally looks much younger) leans from the window with anxious curiosity but remains safely detached, speculating over the intimate drama between his delinquent brother and father. Central to the composition is the father who, seeing his son a long way off, is filled with compassion.

The story of the lost son begs the question: "What does it mean to be 'at home' in the presence of the Father?" The great paradox tucked between the lines of this well-known parable is that in the end, it is the derelict brother who is found in the father's presence, not the older, more dutiful, brother who stayed behind but remained a frustrated child in his own home. Is the crucial difference between the two brothers simply that one lived recklessly and the other did not? Well, maybe. But perhaps the greater difference is that the younger brother saw with convincing clarity the absolute destitution of his life apart from grace and was fortunate enough to find his way home. Whereas the older brother never understood his need of grace because he was deluded by his own ability to maintain dutiful appearances.

The parable suggests that more than anything related to location, "home" belongs to those who realize their need of grace and are humble, courageous or desperate enough to cast themselves into the arms of Christ. The story tells the truth that every Lenten traveler discovers sooner or later: it makes no difference if we "appear" to be self-sufficient and securely at home in this life; if we reside apart from the open embrace of God we are homeless indeed.

Caravaggio
The Incredulity of Thomas

    Thomas discovered something very important about the journey home: namely, that faith is crucial for our appreciation of Christ's presence. When the reality of God's presence is not viscerally perceived, faith protects us from misinterpreting his silence for lack of interest or abandonment. Faith, as Thomas discovered, reminds us that once drawn into the community of God's triune love we can never again accurately say that "we are alone." Yet if we're honest we know that darkness is sometimes substituted for light, and that our experience of God's "felt presence" is often replaced by his "felt absence." Faith reorients our understanding of "presence" when circumstances seem to be divinely turned on their hand. We need faith for the times when God removes the path of illuminated clarity so that we might discover his glory in dark places; when he draws our babbling to a frustrating end in order to draw from us a simple and authentic "yes," and when he allows us to perceive his distance in order to mature our appreciation of his presence.

    At times God seems to answer our desires for knowledge, control and comfort with mystery, frustration and a profound sense of our individual weakness. This happens not that we might learn particular lessons, although we might. What these experiences do is make us uncomfortably aware of our uniqueness before God—an experience easily interpreted as isolation or aloneness. As created persons we live with the tension of being unable to exist as self-sufficient individuals on the one hand, while being equally unable to lose ourselves in God on the other. God intends that we be uniquely ourselves before him, which requires both our freedom and dependence. As children of God we will only experience the sweetness of our human freedom in relation to Him. So while it is the purpose of the Spirit to affirm our individual uniqueness, it is also his purpose to draw us as free persons into loving communion with him.

St. Thomas Didymus

But when my hand
               led by his hand's firm grasp
entered the unhealed wound

              my fingers encountering

rib bone and pulsing heat,

              what I felt was not

scalding pain, shame for

              my obstinate need

but light, light streaming

              into me, over me, filling the room

as if I had lived till then

              in a cold cave, and now

coming forth for the first time

              the knot that bound me unraveling

I witnessed

           all things quicken to color, to form

my question

           not answered but given its part
in a vast unfolding design lit

              by a risen sun

—Denise Levertov

My shepherd is the Living Lord

1. My shep-herd is the liv-ing Lord, noth-ing there-fore I need;
2. When I walk thro' the shades of death, your pres-ence is my stay;
3. The sure pro-vi-sions of my God at-tend me all my days;

in pas-tures fair, near pleas-ant streams you set-tle me to feed.
a word of your sup-port-ing breath drives all my fear a-way.
O may your house be mine abode and all my work be praise.

You bring my wan-dring spir-it back when I for-sake your ways,
Your hand, in sight of all my foes, does still my ta-ble spread;
There would I find a set-tled rest, while oth-ers come and go —

and lead me for your mer-cy's sake in paths of truth and grace.
my cup with bless-ings o-ver flows, your oil a-noints my head.
no more a strang-er or a guest, but like a child at home.

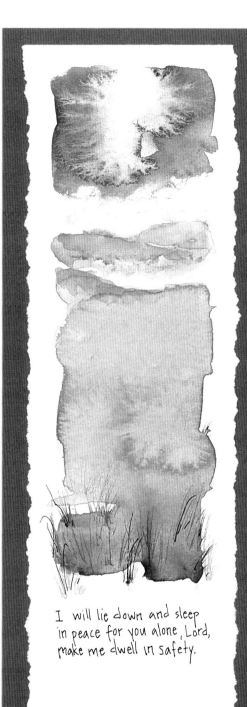

I will lie down and sleep
in peace for you alone, Lord,
make me dwell in safety.

The Abundance of Joy

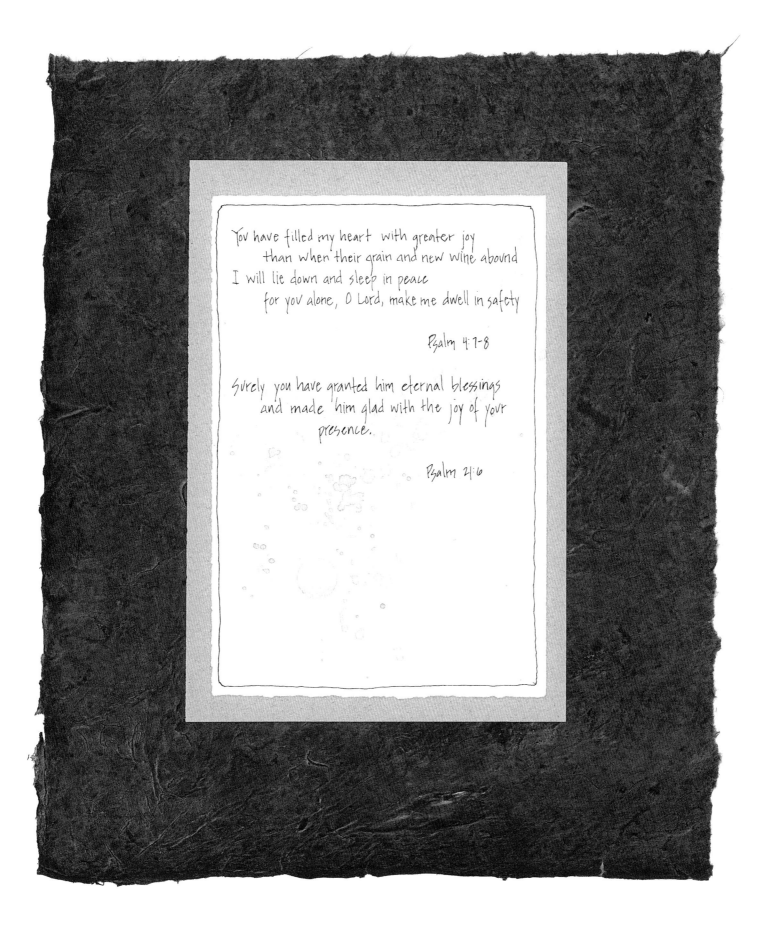

You have filled my heart with greater joy
    than when their grain and new wine abound
I will lie down and sleep in peace
    for you alone, O Lord, make me dwell in safety

                              Psalm 4:7-8

Surely you have granted him eternal blessings
    and made him glad with the joy of your
    presence.

                              Psalm 21:6

"Here is a boy with five small barley loaves and two small fish, but how far will they go among so many?" Jesus said, "have the people sit down." There was plenty of grass in that place, and the men sat down, about five thousand of them. Jesus then took the loaves, gave thanks, and distributed to those who were seated as much as they wanted. He did the same with the fish. When they had all had enough to eat, he said to his disciples, "Gather the pieces that are left over. Let nothing be wasted." So they gathered them and filled twelve baskets with the pieces of the five barley loaves left over by those who had eaten.

John 6:9-13

Joy is the experience of christ's redeeming presence. Who then are the joyful? Rarely in Scripture is it the affluent or successful. Rather, the joyful and blessed are a curious lot: Blessed are the poor, blessed are the meek, blessed are the hungry, blessed are the persecuted. As we have already seen, it was for the impoverished son that the father threw a party. Is there something wryly or mysteriously advantageous about the conditions of poverty and destitution? Whatever the truth may be, there is no getting around the fact that Jesus holds a special place for the weak and marginalized. Joy seems to be the inheritance of those who have responded to the invitation: "Come unto me all ye that labor and are heavy laden."

Lent teaches us that while joy is available to all people, it is most noticeably the property of those who have suffered and known redemption. Jesus himself said, "he who has been forgiven little loves little." Joy, and the abundance of it, are the natural overflow of christ's redemptive presence in a person's life. It is not an imputed emotion, but the experience of wholeness that results when a forgiven person is led beyond their stifling self-consciousness toward communion with God and others.

The angel announced the incarnation of Christ with these words: "I bring good news of great joy that will be for all people. Today a Savior has been born to you; he is Christ the Lord." To receive the Savior is to receive joy. It is to know God's presence, which for us will always be an experience of redemption. For Christ, joy was to do the will of the Father, which meant restoring the creation to proper relationship with God. "Who for the joy set before him endured the cross." Joy is fundamentally a word about relationship. It has little to do with what we possess and everything to do with being loved. Joy knows nothing of fixing ourselves up or making ourselves impressive. It simply means the homecoming of our hearts into the open presence of God. As with the lost son, it is the experience of being welcomed home in spite of ourselves.

Realizing this, we should expect that the journey of Lent will never deliver us to a plateau of power. Rather it will consistently lead us back to the powerlessness of the Lamb. God's ecology of grace dictates that joy will often sprout from dubious soil. From experiences of loss, frustration of desire and shattered dignity emerge new and intimate encounters of his graceful presence. In these encounters he speaks to us: "Do not fear, little flock . . . do not worry about your life." For when we have the Good shepherd, what else could we need?

Albrecht Dürer
Peasants Dancing

Why should cross and trial grieve me?
Need I fear?
Christ is near,
never will he leave me.
Who can rob me of the heaven
that God's son
for my own
to my faith has given.

one

All who in the Lord are planted
should appear everywhere
everywhere
hopeful and undaunted.
Even death cannot apall them:
they rejoice
when the voice
of their Lord doth call them.

two

Lord, my life and joy for ever,
thou art mine,
I am thine,
nothing can us sever.
I am thine, for thou hast bought me;
lost I stood
but thy salvation brought me.

three

Thou art mine; I love and own thee
Light of joy,
ne'er shall I
from my heart dethrone thee.
Saviour, let me soon behold thee
face to face
may thy grace
evermore enfold me.

four

Jesus Christ The Apple Tree

The tree of life my soul hath seen,
Laden with fruit, and always green:
The trees of nature fruitless be
Compared with Christ the apple tree.

His beauty doth all things excel:
By faith I know, but ne'er can tell
The glory which I now can see
In Jesus Christ the apple tree.

For happiness I long have sought,
And pleasure dearly I have bought:
I missed of all; but now I see
'Tis found in Christ the apple tree.

I'm weary with my former toil,
Here I will sit and rest awhile:
Under the shadow I will be,
Of Jesus Christ the apple tree.

This fruit doth make my soul to thrive,
It keeps my dying faith alive;
Which makes my soul in haste to be
With Jesus Christ the apple tree.

My God,
I pray that I may so know and love you
    that I may rejoice in you.
And if I may not do so fully in this life
    let me go steadily on to the day
    I come to that fulness.
Let your love grow in me here,
    and there let it be fulfilled.
So that here my joy may be in a great
    hope, and there in full reality.

St. Anselm (1033-1109)

The Movement Outward

With my mouth I will greatly extol the Lord,
    in the great throng I will praise him.
For he stands at the right hand of the needy one,
    to save his life from those who condemn him.

Psalm 109:30-31

It was just before the Passover Feast. Jesus knew that the time had come for him to leave this world and go to the Father. Having loved his own who were in the world, he now showed them the full extent of his love.

The evening meal was being served, and the devil had already prompted Judas Iscariot, son of Simon, to betray Jesus. Jesus knew that the Father had put all things under his power, and that he had come from God and was returning to God; so he got up from the meal, took off his outer clothing, and wrapped a towel around his waist. After that he poured water into a basin and began to wash his disciples' feet, drying them with the towel that was wrapped around him.

He came to Simon Peter, who said to him, "Lord, are you going to wash my feet?" Jesus replied, "You do not realize now what I am doing, but later you will understand."

"No," said Peter, "you shall never wash my feet."

Jesus answered, "Unless I wash you, you have no part with me."

"Then, Lord," Simon Peter replied, "not just my feet but my hands and my head as well!"

Jesus answered, "A person who has had a bath needs only to wash his feet; his whole body is clean. And you are clean, though not every one of you." For he knew who was going to betray him, and that was why he said not every one was clean.

When he had finished washing their feet, he put on his clothes and returned to his place. "Do you understand what I have done for you?" he asked them. "You call me 'Teacher' and 'Lord', and rightly so, for that is what I am. Now that I, your Lord and Teacher, have washed your feet, you also should wash one another's feet. I have set you an example that you should do as I have done for you. I tell you the truth, no servant is greater than his master, nor is a messenger greater than the one who sent him. Now that you know these things, you will be blessed if you do them.

John 13:1-17

After three years of self-giving love, one symbolic demonstration of compassion remained before Jesus would offer himself completely on behalf of the creation. Jesus knew that all authority had been given to him by his Father. The disciples also knew that Jesus possessed divine authority because he had commanded the elements, diseases and evil spirits on so many previous occasions. Now at the high point of the disciples' confidence in the authority of Jesus, he does a very peculiar thing: he begins, one at a time, to wash their feet. In so doing, Jesus reverses every assumption that might have been held about the rights and privileges of power as well as the very nature of love.

"Do you understand what I've done for you?" This is the question Jesus puts to the beleaguered disciples after washing their feet. That same question, "Do you understand what I've done for you?" has not stopped echoing through the hearts of men and women since Jesus first asked it. Do we understand? Have we caught the smallest glimpse of what it means for the Christ of creation to wash the feet of common people – people like ourselves? Has the magnitude of his compassion penetrated our composure? Has his love broken the hard shell of our guilty conscience?

This story is one of those rare occasions in which Jesus chooses to explain the mystery created by his own behavior. After he makes it clear that, in fact, the disciples do not realize what he has done, he tells them: "Now that I, your Lord and teacher have washed your feet, you also should wash one another's feet." The explanation reveals at least two things about the nature of God's love. First, God's love proceeds by action. As Bernard of Clairvaux once said, "we must remember that love reveals itself, not by words or phrases, but by action and experience." Second, authority and power do not exclude us from serving one another, but rather employ us to serve others.

How is it that two simple objects, a bowl of water and a towel, come to symbolize the magnitude of Christ's love? Because in them we see Christ reaching for instruments of service rather than instruments of power. But while the miracles demonstrated his love, they were open to misinterpretation as mere acts of power. There is no misunderstanding this final act, however. It is a demonstration of sheer humility. When Jesus, in all his authority, serves his disciples by washing their feet, the magnitude of his love is realized. Through his openness and undiscriminating movement towards others in service, we know the love of God.

Rembrandt van Rijn
Christ Washing the Disciples' Feet

For us, the imperative to serve one another and live outwardly has a foundation far deeper than mere social virtue. It is an invitation to be who we were created to be, made in the image of the triune God. As the Father, Son and Spirit co-exist in a dance of mutual indwelling, so the image of God is fulfilled in our lives when we live openly and outwardly — participating in the life around us with acts of love.

But, the Lenten journey is not over. We have not yet followed Christ to the end. When Jesus asks Peter "Do you love me?" it is the command which follows Peter's confession that is so intriguing. "Feed my sheep," Jesus says. It's as if Jesus is saying to Peter, "I've shown you what it means to love. Now be true to the love you've confessed and do as I have done." After telling Peter to care for his sheep, Jesus warns him that his hands will be tied and that he'll be taken where he does not want to go — indicating the kind of death Peter would die. It should come as no surprise to us that following Jesus will regularly lead us to places where we would rather not go — to places we've spent our whole lives trying to avoid. The journey of Lent unremittingly confronts us with the paradox which lies at the heart of the christian story: That the cross, while a symbol of life, is first and foremost an instrument of death. Only after the cross served its life-stealing function was it converted into a life-giving symbol.

An upper room did our Lord prepare
for those he loved until the end:
and his disciples still gather there
to celebrate their risen friend.

A lasting gift Jesus gave his own:
to share his bread, his living cup.
Whatever burdens may bow us down,
he by his cross shall lift us up.

And after supper he washed their feet,
for service, too, is sacrament,
In him our joy shall be made complete —
sent out to serve, as he was sent.

No end there is! We depart in peace.
He loves beyond our uttermost:
In every room in our Father's house
he will be there, as Lord and host.

Lord, make me an instrument of your peace. Where there is hatred, let me sow love; where there is injury, pardon; where there is doubt, faith; where there is despair, hope; where there is darkness, light; where there is sadness, joy.

O divine Master, grant that I may not so much seek to be consoled, as to console; to be understood, as to understand; to be loved, as to love. For it is in giving that we receive; it is in pardoning that we are pardoned; and it is in dying that we are born to eternal life. Amen.

St. Francis

The Final Act

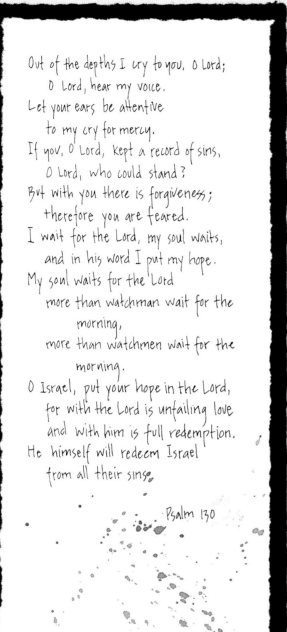

Out of the depths I cry to you, O Lord;
   O Lord, hear my voice.
Let your ears be attentive
   to my cry for mercy.
If you, O Lord, kept a record of sins,
   O Lord, who could stand?
But with you there is forgiveness;
   therefore you are feared.
I wait for the Lord, my soul waits,
   and in his word I put my hope.
My soul waits for the Lord
      more than watchman wait for the
         morning,
      more than watchmen wait for the
         morning.
O Israel, put your hope in the Lord,
   for with the Lord is unfailing love
   and with him is full redemption.
He himself will redeem Israel
   from all their sins.

                              Psalm 130

Then the disciples went back to their homes, but Mary stood outside the tomb crying. As she wept, she bent over to look into the tomb and saw two angels in white, seated where Jesus' body had been, one at the head and the other at the foot.

They asked her, "Woman, why are you crying?"

"They have taken my Lord away," she said, "and I don't know where they have put him." At this, she turned around and saw Jesus standing there, but she did not realize that it was Jesus.

"Woman," he said, "why are you crying? Who is it you are looking for?"

Thinking he was the gardener, she said, "Sir, if you have carried him away, tell me where you have put him, and I will get him."

Jesus said to her, "Mary."

She turned toward him and cried out in Aramaic, "Rabboni!" (which means Teacher).

matthias Grünewald
Isenheimer Alter

Reading John's account of the Passion we are struck by the sheer physicality of the narrative. The closing days of Jesus' life are woven together by a string of personality profiles and sensate descriptions. A swarm of lanterns glint in the darkness, soldiers with weapons approach the olive grove, a servant's ear is severed, small fires dull the bite of the cool, night air, early morning interviews are punctuated with beatings, a rooster crows judgment, and blood-letting mockery pierces the brow of Jesus. All of this detail precedes the vivid brutality of the crucifixion.

Of the many vignettes exhibited in the passion there must be at least one scene perfectly suited to each one of us. Some of us are companions to Peter, cowering in the shadows, afraid of being identified with Jesus. Others identify with Pilate, asking practical questions like: "What is truth?" when truth is the person looking us in the face. Still others weep with Mary Magdalene at the tomb, conferring with "gardeners" until The Gardener calls them by name.

Whoever we are, the momentum of Lent draws each of us to the same Easter climax ~ to the company of him who invites, compels and solicits our love. We acknowledged at the beginning of our journey that Christ would draw us to the Trinity from within and that he would not leave us to ourselves to search him out.

The death and resurrection of Christ have established this truth forever. When Christ is crucified he experiences the depths of what it means to be a creature in a fallen world. He suffers death because death is the judgment that belongs to sin.

But even though death is clearly God's judgment on sin, the goal of that judgment is to bring sin and suffering to an end; which is precisely why the incarnation is such good news. By taking on our humanity Christ suffers sin's judgment in order that through him evil and pain might be finally robbed of its power. His suffering is no charade. When he speaks the words "My God, my God, why have you forsaken me?" he asks the question familiar to us all. When he sweats drops of blood we know his agony is real. By faith we realize that Jesus will not leave us alone in our suffering. In his earthly life and death, Christ identifies with us. This gives us great comfort. But the triumph of Easter is that in the resurrection we are identified with Christ. The implication this has for our suffering is that human pain finds its conclusion in the resurrected Christ. This is not to say that human suffering has, or should, come to an end. It does mean that our present suffering is given meaning in the mercy of Christ. We're not offered explanations, but hope - hope that our suffering is not the end of the story but that Christ is. And when Christ is our end, life has only just begun.

On the morning of his resurrection Jesus tells Mary Magdalene to go and tell the other disciples that he is returning to the Father. But notice that it is not only his Father to whom he is returning. His words are: "I am returning to my Father and your Father, to my God and your God." By the resurrection, our relationship to God is established forever on the basis of Christ's relationship to his Father. The miracle of Easter is the hope of redeemed suffering. It is the hope of forgiven sin. And finally, it is the hope of rediscovering our home in loving communion with the Triune God of all creation.

I Know That My Redeemer Lives

I know that my Redeemer lives —
what joy the blessed assurance gives
He lives, he lives, who once was dead;
He lives, my everlasting Head.

He lives, to bless me with his love;
he lives, to plead for me above;
he lives, my hungry soul to feed;
he lives, to help in time of need.

He lives, and grants me daily breath;
he lives, and I shall conquer death;
he lives, my mansion to prepare;
he lives, to lead me safely there.

He lives, all glory to his name;
he lives, my Savior, still the same;
what joy the blessed assurance gives,
I know that my Redeemer lives!

                           — Samuel Medley

Almighty God,
You have broken the tyranny of sin
and have sent the spirit of your
        Son into our hearts
Whereby we call you Father
Give us grace to dedicate our
        freedom to your service,
that we and all creation may be brought
        to the glorious liberty of
        the children of God,
through Jesus Christ our Lord.

    Amen.

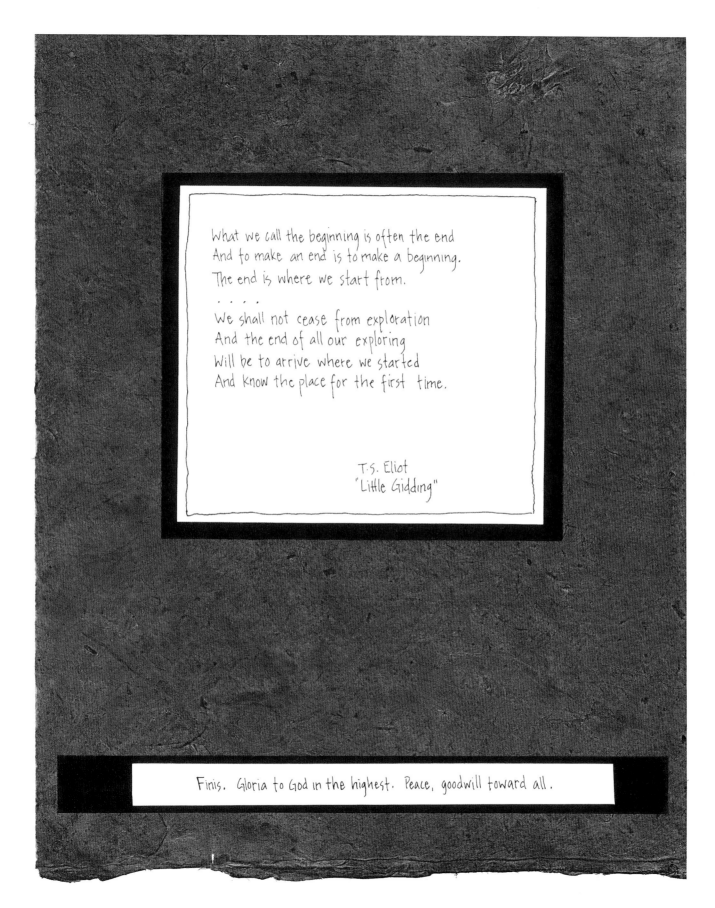

What we call the beginning is often the end
And to make an end is to make a beginning.
The end is where we start from.

. . . .

We shall not cease from exploration
And the end of all our exploring
Will be to arrive where we started
And know the place for the first time.

T.S. Eliot
"Little Gidding"

Finis. Gloria to God in the highest. Peace, goodwill toward all.

Acknowledgements and Notes

The author and publisher acknowledge with thanks permission to reproduce copyright material as listed below. Every effort has been made to trace copyright owners, and the publishers apologize to anyone whose rights have inadvertently not been acknowledged. This will be corrected in any reprint.

Unless noted, Scripture quotations taken from the HOLY BIBLE, NEW INTERNATIONAL VERSION. Copyright 1973, 1978, 1984 by International Bible Society. Used by permission of Zondervan Publishing House Hodder & Stoughten Limited. All rights reserved.

The "NIV" and "New International Version" trademarks are registered in the United States Patent and Trademark Office by International Bible Society. Use of either trademark requires the permission of International Bible Society.

"NIV" is a registered trademark of International Bible Society. UK Trademark number 1448790.

The Invitation

George MacDonald: quoted from Creation in Christ, edited by Rolland Hein. (Harold Shaw Publishers, 1976).

St. Augustine: quoted from The Confessions of St. Augustine, transl. Edward B. Pusey. (Collier Books, 1961).

T.S. Eliot: from "Ash Wednesday," Selected Poems. (Faber and Faber, 1975).

Rublev: Icon of the Old Testament Trinity. (Scala/Art Resource, NY).

Prayer, from the Book of Common Prayer. © 1962 by the General Synod of the Anglican Church of Canada. Published by the Anglican Book Centre. Used with permission.

George Herbert: "Love (3)", The Church. (Alfred A. Knopf, 1995).

R. Vaughn Williams: Five Mystical Songs. Reproduced by permission of Stainer and Bell Ltd., London, England.

The Desert of Temptation

Masaccio: Expulsion from Paradise. (Scala/Art Resource, NY).

William Blake: I want, I want. Used with permission of the Fitzwilliam Museum, Cambridge, England.

John Chrysostom: quoted from The Communion of Saints: Prayers of the Famous, edited by Horton Davies. (Eerdmans, 1990).

John Donne: quoted from The Divine Poems, edited by Helen Gardner. (Oxford University Press, 1966).

Uncovering Illusions

Georges Rouault: Don't We All Wear Make-Up? © 2000 Verwertungsgesellschaft Bildender Künstler
    (VBK), Vienna/ADAGP, Paris.
W.H. Auden: "The Age of Anxiety, A Baroque Eclogue," from Part 6: The Epilogue, Collected Longer
    Poems. (Vintage Books, 1975).
Georges Rouault: The Wounded Clown I. © 2000 Verwertungsgesellschaft Bildender Künstler
    (VBK), Vienna/ADAGP, Paris.
Fabrice Hergott, transl. Richard Rees: Rouault. (Ediciones Poligrafa, S.A.: 1991).
T.S. Eliot: "Little Gidding" in FOUR QUARTETS, © 1942 by T.S. Eliot and renewed 1970 by Esme Valerie
    Eliot, reprinted by permission of the publishers Harcourt, Inc. and Faber and Faber.
Lucien Diess, C.S.Sp., transl. Matthew J. OConnell: "The Anaphoras of Addai and Mari", Springtime of
    the Liturgy. (The Liturgical Press, 1979).

The Abiding Presence

Rembrandt van Rijn: The Return of the Prodigal Son. Used by permission of The Pierpont Morgan Library,
    New York, B.91, RvR 143.
Caravaggio: Incredulity of St. Thomas. (Scala/Art Resource, NY).
Denise Levertov: "St. Thomas Didymus", A Door in the Hive. © 1989 by Denise Levertov. Reprinted by
    kind permission of New Directions Publishing Corp, New York, and Laurence Pollinger Limited, London.
"My Shepherd is the Living Lord". Words by Thomas Sternhold (1549) and Isaac Watts (1719). American
    folk harmony by Erik Routley.

The Abundance of Joy

Albrecht Dürer: The Peasant Couple Dancing (Engraving, 1514). Used by permission of The Metropolitan
    Museum of Art, Fletcher Fund, 1919.
"Why Should Cross and Trial Grieve Me?" Probable authors, Paul Gerhardt and Johann G. Ebeling.
    Copyright control.
Joshua Smith (1784): "Jesus Christ the Apple Tree."
Saint Anselm: from the "Proslogion," a modern translation.

The Movement Outward

Fred Pratt Green: "An Upper Room." Words © 1974, Hope Publishing Company. Carol Stream, IL 60188.
    All rights reserved. Used by permission.
"Prayer of St. Francis." Attributed to St. Francis of Assisi.

The Final Act

Matthias Grünewald: <u>The Issenheim Alter</u>. (Erich Lessing / Art Resource, NY).

Georges Rouault: <u>The Apparition</u>. © 2000 Verwertungsgesellschaft Bildender Künstler (VBK), Vienna / ADAGP, Paris.

Samuel Medley: "I Know That My Redeemer Lives."

T.S. Eliot: "Little Gidding" in FOUR QUARTETS, © 1942 by T.S. Eliot and renewed 1970 by Esme Valerie Eliot, reprinted by permission of the publishers Harcourt, Inc. and Faber and Faber.

George Herbert: <u>The Church</u>, closing lines.